MANNERIST PAINTING SIXTEENTH CENTURY

MANNERIST PAINTING

THE SIXTEENTH CENTURY

by Kurt Forster
Yale University

McGRAW-HILL BOOK COMPANY
New York   Toronto   London   Sydney

MANNERIST PAINTING

European painting between Renaissance and Baroque has too many different facets to be conveniently grouped under one heading, but its dominant trend — Mannerism — demands a comparative study. North and south of the Alps this new art contradicted Renaissance principles in its expressive licenses, its often willfully daring color, distorting proportions and ambiguous spatial setting. Compositional intricacies replaced the earlier balance of all elements, and complicated poses and emotional affectation increased the complexities further.

The term Mannerism was originally applied to the art of Michelangelo's followers and imitators, but during recent decades has been stretched into an all inclusive label for sixteenth-century Italian as well as European art in general. In a positive sense, the modern concept of Mannerism takes its precise definition from a small group of artists in Florence and Rome who began during the teens and twenties of the sixteenth century to challenge the exclusive and normative values of the art of Raphael and some of his contemporaries.

Leonardo's *Mona Lisa*, Raphael's Madonnas and Sarto's frescoes and altarpieces must have appeared too balanced, too harmoniously resolved within themselves for the doubting, searching and introspective eyes of early Mannerist painters. Pontormo, Rosso Fiorentino, Giulio Romano and others reacted against the dignified aims and the ever finer grain of the High Renaissance ideals a good decade before such catastrophic events as the sack of Rome (1527), the collapse of the Florentine Republic (1530) and the religious wars of the Reformation

3

revealed to everyone the abyss under the very foundations of the Renaissance.

Where the High Renaissance postulated solutions and achieved a harmonious balance — by excluding all elements incapable of such sublimation — Mannerism reaffirmed the questions and demanded recognition of a torn and struggling world thrown off balance by its own contradictory forces. Though the young Mannerist painters broke overtly with the High Renaissance, their revolution was but the final step in the slow evolution of Leonardo and Michelangelo who had already begun to move away from the ideals of their youth. One must look back for a moment in order to perceive at once the continuity and the marked break in the history of Renaissance and Mannerist art.

By 1512 Leonardo, Michelangelo and Raphael had achieved their highly personal styles from which every definition of High Renaissance art has been derived. New, and yet a synthesis of a long development, their works in Milan, Florence and Rome seemed to transform everything else into history. As fifteenth-century artists had learned to think of the world in terms of perspective, symmetry, true proportions and bodily presence, Leonardo and Michelangelo, in their effort to establish an ideal art, animated their figures and made them expressive of individual moods. Hence Leonardo's life-long preoccupation with the inner flux and flow, the "cause of all life," and with the elusive atmosphere at "the fall of the evening when it is cloudy or misty." Hence also Michelangelo's preference for forced poses and strangely engaging but impenetrable facial expressions. As Leonardo and Michelangelo sought to understand more deeply the movement of bodies and the varying moods pervading them, they broke further and further away from the static proportions of Renaissance art. Scholastic and neo-platonic speculations on the eternal rift between the spirit and its bodily cage, between essence and appearance, deepened the growing distrust in the physical nature of things. Beauty was

Figure 1.   Pontormo:
Joseph in Egypt
National Gallery, London

no longer thought to consist in proper perspective and physical ideality, but took on the elusive inward quality of a "divine idea."

During the period of growing spiritual unrest in the later teens of the sixteenth century, the young Florentine painters Pontormo (1494-1556) and Rosso (1495-1540) broke away from the carefully respected boundaries of the Renaissance art of Fra Bartolommeo and Andrea del Sarto, who had both matured under the impact of Raphael's conciliatory art before 1508. Pontormo's rather small painting, *Joseph in Egypt* (1517/18), was commissioned as a decoration for a bridal chamber — a very old-fashioned framework for a painting of such revolutionary significance (Figure 1). Pontormo unfolds two entire chapters from the *Book of Genesis* in five major areas of

Figure 2. Dürer:
Christ before Pilate.
Woodcut from
the "Small Passion"

the panel. The painter's concept of the story accounts for the particular structure of this painting: disparate places and events are joined together as if various unrelated spheres were hurtling toward each other. Some of the strikingly caricaturesque heads, agitated gestures and the completely Northern buildings in the background are derived with minute precision from Lucas van Leyden's print *Ecce Homo* of 1510. This print was a favorite in the Sarto shop and quotations from it appear in several other pictures. Northern prints like Dürer's *Christ before Pilate* (Figure 2) were well studied by Pontormo, who may have been emboldened by their discontinuous settings and emphatic language of silhouette and gesture, as well as by their more literal and violent depiction of Christ's suffering. Significantly, both Pontormo's *Joseph in Egypt* and Dürer's woodcut suppress the main axis as well as any hint of the eye-level.

As early as 1518 Pontormo completely repealed several "dogmas" of Florentine art of his time: he disrupts the unity of the spatial setting and he changes the scale from one area of the picture to another. The impeccable "finish" and uniform tone of High Renaissance pictures give way to a speckled surface of high-keyed, flashing hues. This rupture of unity and pre-established coherence — and hence of the harmony of all parts — gains sharp accents in the jumping levels and interlocked rhythms of steps and stairs. His prodigious contemporary Rosso Fiorentino (who had spent some time with Pontormo in Sarto's shop) gave an even more determined rebuff to High Renaissance ideals with his *Deposition* of 1521 (Color slide 1). Harsh light breaks every surface into hard-edged, jagged planes. Rosso's shapes in loose and sketchy strokes are not unlike Michelangelo's hewn out unfinished figures.

The Florentine manifestations of a new art were paralleled in Rome. Already Michelangelo's *Sistine Ceiling* (1508-12) had progressed from heroic ideality in its earlier sections to much more complex images of figures locked in antagonistic positions and set in ambiguously fragmented places, as in the *Punishment of Haman* in the left corner spandrel above the altar.

If Raphael's first stately room, the *Stanza della Segnatura*, in the new Vatican suite for Pope Julius II clearly established his classical ideal, the two following rooms of *Heliodorus* (1511-14) and of the *Fire in the Borgo* (1514-17) shattered the harmony of his first Roman style (Figure 3). As his work progressed, his chief assistant Giulio Romano (ca. 1499-1546) gained increasing responsibility and a larger share in the actual executions of these frescoes. The *Fire in the Borgo* bears clearly the mark of Giulio's work and most likely it is also largely of his own invention. The balanced and dignified presence which pervades the earlier *School of Athens* has been broken and disrupted in the anguished actions of hurried groups and figures moving through fragmented settings. Stable symmetry is replaced by the counterbalance of uneven and incoherent parts; harmonious presence, by rushed activity.

Figure 3.   Raphael and Giulio Romano: Fire in the Borgo. Stanza dell'Incendio, Vatican

Figure 4. Parmigianino:
Self-Portrait.
Kunsthistorisches Museum,
Vienna

The High Renaissance Rome of Leo X attracted many artists from all over Italy: Beccafumi (1485/6-1551) carried back to provincial Siena a lasting appreciation for the art of Michelangelo. An isolated and independent figure in his hometown, he developed a highly personal style of strangely posed figures painted in melting, glowing colors (Color slide 2). Many artists left Rome after the death of Leo X (1521). Others were driven from the city during the sack of 1527: the introspective Parmigianino — who had presented Pope Clement VII with his *Self-Portrait* (1522/3) painted on a wooden segment to simulate the distorted image of a convex mirror (Figure 4) — returned to Upper Italy; Rosso Fiorentino moved through provincial towns in Umbria and Tuscany, reaching Venice before his emigration to France.

Raphael's pupils and collaborators dispersed early in the twenties and formed new side-branches of Roman Mannerism which excelled particularly in grand fresco-works: Perino del Vaga (1500/1-1547) went to Genoa where he decorated the Palazzo Doria, but later returned to Rome under Pius III to fresco large rooms in the Castel Sant'Angelo. The Genoese painter Luca Cambiaso (1527-85) foreshadows with his somber nightpieces the early Baroque painting of Caravaggio (Color slide 3).

Giulio Romano's own paintings emphasize an increasing preoccupation with sudden and violent events which he depicted in harsh contrasts of light and dark, outlining aggressive gestures as if momentarily arrested by terror. Lacking the patronage, after the death of Leo X, which would allow him to fully realize his theatrical imagination, Giulio accepted an invitation from Federico II Gonzaga, ruler of Mantua. Over the years he established himself as chief architect, painter and artistic director at the court where a tradition of lavish patronage, collecting and loving appreciation of learned and even esoteric art ensured his success. For his most important assignment, the construction of the summer residence *Palazzo del Te* outside the city gates, Giulio enclosed two courtyards with a low building quadrangle and extending walls linked by a colonnaded exedra. Rough and smooth, rule and fancy intermingle in an architectural design which thrives on ambiguities and puns, where triglyphs drop from their proper positions, and the metrum of even bays is broken by visual syncopation. Little was to follow after Giulio's death while his early activities were paralleled in Bologna, Parma and Mantua by the ever more haunted elegance of Parmigianino's altarpieces and frescoes. At the Castle of Fontanellato (1523), Parmigianino had worked from Correggio's example of the Convent of S. Paolo at Parma towards a refined fluidity of the brush and an ecstatically sublimated elegance in his asymmetrical compositions (Color slide 4).

In 1550 Vasari published the first modern history of the arts with his *Lives of the Most Eminent Architects, Sculptors and Painters,* and later revised and amplified the second edition of 1568. The exemplary nature of his work lies not only in its value as a prime source book but as much in its theory of history and style that lastingly impressed itself on later writers. Vasari wished to demonstrate the revival of the true art of the ancients in Giotto's work, its gradual perfection during the fifteenth century and its final consummation in Michelangelo who even surpassed the art of Antiquity. The artists of Vasari's own home province of Tuscany were seen as the main originators of the new art. Like Giulio Romano, Vasari was also a collector, especially of drawings, which he assembled on album pages in collage-like fashion held together by ornamental border and frame designs by his own hand. Even here one may find again some of the principles of Mannerist art: a whole cleverly pieced together from alien fragments, as well as a new historical awareness of the artist's own time and of his place in the development of the arts.

Like Giulio Romano at Mantua, other architects designed

ville for aristocrats and the clergy in many parts of Italy. Genga built the Villa Imperiale near Pesaro (1530-40); Vignola designed the majestic structure at Caprarola (1558-62) on an old hexagonal fortification, and the villa for Pope Julius III (1551-55) at Rome. The Medici called on Ammanati to enlarge their Pitti Palace and lay out the Boboli Gardens. Sanmicheli (1484-1559) was active in Verona and Venice, and Palladio (1508-80) combined in his preciously calculated designs for town and country houses (in and around Vicenza), a systematic knowledge of antique architecture with a new sense for speculative proportional harmonies. All of these *ville* and *palazzi* were to be decorated with elaborately programmed frescoes, such as Giulio Romano's work at Mantua (Color slide 5).

During the turbulent last years of the Florentine republic (1527-30) Pontormo had painted such unique pictures as his *Deposition* (Color slide 6). But after the Emperor and Pope instituted the Duchy of Tuscany under Medici rule (1532) he labored mainly on uncongenial decorations. In the thirties his pupil Bronzino (1503-72) gained particular favor with elaborate, compositionally contrived works of enamel-like finish as the *Portrait of Ugolino Martelli* (Color slide 7) and *Allegory of Love* (Figure 5) which Cosimo I presented to the king of France.

Small studios offered a welcome, if melancholy, escape from the ever more stilted officiality of a court life now essentially Spanish in dress and ceremony throughout Western Europe. Vasari gave to Francesco de' Medici's *studiolo* (1570-71) the familiar touch of his and his patron's taste for the precious and abstruse. With a *grotto* (1583) erected in the Boboli Gardens by Buontalenti another favorite note was struck (Figure 6). Since Raphael and Giulio Romano had begun to use antique *grotteschi* designs in the Papal apartment and in the Villa Madama in Rome, as well as actual shells and pebbles for bathrooms and rustic grottos, these became customary in every villa and formal garden of the century. But special meaning was given to the Boboli grotto by placing two of Michelangelo's unfinished statues in the corners of this artificial "cave" where water sprinkled over porous incrustations. The roughly hewn blocks of Michelangelo's unfinished *Slaves* merge with the tufa of the grotto as if they were chained to the raw and lowly stuff of nature. This was hardly Michelangelo's own understanding but nevertheless a significant hint at the fashionable cult of the grotto and the new antinomy which divided nature and art.

If many of Michelangelo's sculptural figures seem to emerge from the stone in a painful process of individuation, the contrasts of rough and smooth, of calculated and accidental elements were later brought to decorative play in many pieces of sculpture. Giovanni da Bologna (1529-1608), who was trained in Flanders, carved a *Jupiter Pluviale*, over one-hundred feet tall, from a grown rock at Pratolino (near Florence), as well as the intricately calculated group of the *Rape of the Sabine Women*. (1579-83). He went beyond Cellini's criterion of eight well-planned views for a sculpture seen at angles of forty-five degrees during the spectator's full circle around it (Figure 7). Giovanni da Bologna's group arrests the high point of violent struggle in a perfectly calculated composition of diagonals rotating around the unarticulated vertical axis. Differing from the fifteenth-century suggestion of movement through posture and agitated silhouette as much as from the Baroque release of movement as the inherent state of things, the *Rape of the Sabine* epitomizes again a typically Mannerist concept in its coincidence of action and arrest.

Michelangelo returned to Rome for good in 1534 to begin the *Last Judgment* (Figure 8) which the unfortunate Pope Clement VII had commissioned shortly before his death. Michelangelo arrived in a city still marked by neglect and destruction from the sack of 1527. Since the 1540's, not least through his association with the religious reformers around Valdès, Vittoria Colonna, Caterina Cybò and a group of Cardinals, Michelangelo came to understand in his most personal terms the universal significance of Christ's self-sacrifice and of his redeeming grace. Like Pontormo before him, he turned a commission for two frescoes in the Papal chapel (1542-50) of the Vatican (the *Pauline Chapel*) into intense new visions

Figure 8. Michelangelo: Last Judgment (central part). Sistine Chapel, Vatican

(Color slide 8) of long established themes. The innermost meaning of each event was cast into metaphorical shape. None of Michelangelo's later works were completed during his lifetime or were indeed completable in the terms on which he had begun them. It is highly significant that Michelangelo carried the dialectic of "concept" and embodiment to a point where, in his own words, "one would not think how much blood it costs" to give shape to the inner image through the inert matter of the stone.

During the fifteenth century Italian artists responded occasionally to Late Gothic art of the North, but Pontormo was the first to abandon, under the impact of Dürer's graphic art, the Renaissance concept of a heroic Christ; and instead he was to render the suffering, mocked and tortured Son of Man in the monumental frescoes (1523-25) in the cloister of the Certosa near Florence. Titian for his magnificent *Ecce Homo* (Figure 9) of 1543, and later Tintoretto (1518-94) in the *Scuola di San Rocco* (Color slide 10) drew on Dürer's prints for their figures of Christ.

Since Giorgione, Venetian painting stands apart in its character and consistent development toward a reconciliation of mind and nature, of form and color, as much as in its love for lavish display and ceremonial pageantry. Titian and Tintoretto climaxed Venetian art in that they constituted everything through the glow and flicker of color and tone rather than through abstracted design. Titian's handling of paint itself on rough-textured canvas, amalgamating and modulating tones with his fingers, was later to teach Rubens as much as Renoir (Color slide 11). The ecstatic art of the Cretan Domenikos Theotocopoulos, called El Greco, matured through longer training in Venice where no one single artist among the many he knew must have impressed him as strongly as Tintoretto.

The kind of metaphorical meaning to which Michelangelo plied his images appealed to patrons and theorists even if

they frequently preferred a more obvious kind of symbolism wedded to expansive programs. Benedetto Varchi explained a poem by Michelangelo to the academicians in Florence (1546), later requesting their opinion on the superiority of sculpture or painting. In spite of much narcisistic learning Varchi came up with a keen definition of art: "Art is a productive activity with true comprehension for those things which are not necessary. The principle of a work of art lies not in its objects but in him who makes it." Art is riveted in the inner *idea* through which the artist conceives of the true nature of his objects.

Much of the appeal of art theory may well have come from the aspirations of artists since Leonardo's time to be considered on a par with philosophers rather than to remain in the class of artisans to which they had belonged for many centuries. Guilds and patterns of training were slowly broken by the emergence of independent and unruly minds like Leonardo, Michelangelo, Pontormo and Rosso, among many; and associations of artists, more expressive of their new stature, were founded under aristocratic patronage. Bandinelli first grouped students in Rome, and around the middle of the century, in Florence; Vasari founded the Florentine Academy of Design in 1562, and Ludovico Carracci opened an academy in Bologna in 1585/6. Elevating the arts from the mechanical to the level of the liberal arts, the canonic function of these institutions tended in the same direction as the more dogmatic publications on architecture (Vignola, *The Rules of the Five Orders of Architecture*, 1562); sculpture (Danti, *Treatise on Perfect Proportions*, 1567; Cellini, *Two Treatises on Engraving and Sculpture*, 1568); and painting (Lomazzo, *Treatise on the Art of Painting*, 1584; Armenini, *The Proper Rules of Painting*, 1587), which underscore the increasing stabilization in all sectors of social and artistic activity after the mid-century.

Following the death of Michelangelo (1564), Cellini (1571), Bronzino (1572), Titian (1576), Veronese (1588) and Tintoretto (1594), Italian art went through a short period of drought in which only the classicizing art of the Carracci School formed an oasis in Bologna. Reni, Domenichino and Guercino, the formative painters of the early seventeenth century were to emerge from their shop. With Caravaggio's maturation after 1600 and Bernini's new sculpture of energetic movement in the 1620's, the antinomies of Mannerist art were broken up by the originators of the Roman Baroque.

The history of Mannerist art in Europe at large presents diverse and complex problems. The central issue revolves around the reception and absorption of Italian art into the various native traditions. Intense contacts were established through traveling artists, exchange of works and — with remarkable speed — through the wide diffusion of prints. But Italian High Renaissance art had barely received attention outside of Italy when a much stronger impact was made by early Mannerism. In its unclassical character, Mannerist art was often more easily accessible to Northerners than the serene achievements of the High Renaissance. Emigrant artists — Rosso, Primaticcio, Tibaldi, Zuccaro and many others — founded influential schools outside of their homeland, but soon the further developments were strongly diversified and varying in speed. Granting the overall similarity and historical kinship of the various national Mannerist styles, the different countries and regions soon moved "out of phase," as it were, and hence require more detailed attention.

Art in the German-speaking countries was still predominantly Late Gothic at the beginning of the sixteenth century. Before High Renaissance ideals found wider acceptance in the North, artists like Grünewald, Altdorfer and others developed a highly emotional and intricate style quite comparable to Early Italian Mannerism. Their works are characterized by a calligraphically fluid, often mesh-like brushwork and strongly expressive coloration. From Late Gothic traditions they acquired a violent intensity of expression hardly ever tolerated in the South, and not shared by their contemporaries Dürer and Holbein the Younger.

Dürer returned to Nuremberg after his second trip to Venice in 1505/6 with the intention of creating an art in the North equal to that of his admired Giovanni Bellini. This classicizing aim was opposed by his contemporary Mathias Gothardt, called Grünewald (ca. 1470-1528), who is in many respects Dürer's artistic antipode: certainly familiar with the Italian Renaissance, he did not Italianize his art but made it singularly expressive of his intense vision, melting late-Gothic imagery in a new metaphorical reality. His major work, the *Isenheim Altar* (ca. 1512-15), reaches from the ghastly figure of the Crucified in front of a dark sky to the jubilantly glowing colors of the Madonna in the Heavenly temple; from the murky monsters torturing St. Anthony to the revelation of divine light in the *Resurrection of Christ* (Color slide 12). A phenomenal kinship to Pontormo's and Beccafumi's later works (Color slides 6, 2) is established by the equally melting, waxen colors of an un-

Figure 10. Urs Graf:
Soldiers in a Landscape.
Printroom, Public Art Collection
Basel

Figure 11. Altdorfer:
The Battle of
Alexander and Darius.
Alte Pinakothek
Munich

earthly glow. These diaphanous figures in a supernatural light defy ordinary classification in the terms which the Renaissance proposed. There is no mutual influence here, but Grünewald's, Pontormo's and Beccafumi's works share a similar historical position: they declare the insufficiency of self-contained, plastic figures.

Some of Albrecht Altdorfer's (ca. 1480-1538) paintings, for example, his *Resurrection of Christ* (1518), convey a similarly emotional coloration and expressive shaping of figures usually set in the finely meshed, abundant growth of nature. Altdorfer painted and etched the first pure landscapes; Dürer before him had watercolored alpine views along his way to Venice, and Lucas Cranach (1472-1553) had given an unusually prominent role to the landscapes in both his religious paintings and his portraits, since his stay in Vienna early in the sixteenth century. Cranach, Altdorfer and Wolf Huber (1485-1553) are often grouped in the so-called "Danube School" since they shared a predominant interest in landscape painting. But otherwise their association must have been very loose. The Swiss goldsmith, draftsman and engraver Urs Graf (ca. 1485-1527/8) spent most of his life in Basle when he was not campaigning with the mercenaries. His marvelously fluid, calligraphic draftsmanship captures many unheroic moments of military life and misfortune in an often brutal frankness. His landscapes emerge from swirling dashes of the pen that link him with Altdorfer and Wolf Huber (Figure 10).

In 1528 when he was city architect in Regensburg, Altdorfer refused the position of burgomaster in order to put his whole energy into a commission from the Duke of Bavaria for the *Battle of Alexander and Darius* (Figure 11 and Color slide 13). In contrast to Italian history painting, e.g. Leonardo's and Michelangelo's projected battle scenes in the Palazzo Vecchio (Florence) or the Vatican frescoes of early Christian history in Raphael's *Stanze,* Altdorfer does not focus on a group of classi-

Figure 12.   Adrien de Vries:
Bust of Emperor Rudolph II.
Kunsthistorisches Museum,
Vienna

cal figures in a crucial confrontation. He lifts the observer's eye high above the earth and lets the squadrons of lancers clash below like windswept wheatfields while the view extends to the curved, ice-blue horizon under a swirling vulcan of clouds around the rising sun.

Grünewald's sympathy with Lutheran ideas cost him the patronage of the Catholic prince-bishop of Mainz whereas Lucas Cranach, a personal friend of the reformer, enjoyed the protection of the protestant electors of Saxony for whom his large shop produced portraits, religious paintings and a particular kind of mythological picture (Color slide 14).

In prosperous banking and trading centers, wealthy families like the Fugger in Augsburg patronized artists and skilled craftsmen, but the archducal collections in Ambras (near Innsbruck), Graz and Prague, and their princely counterparts in Munich, Heidelberg and elsewhere, had often been assembled with a taste more for wayward curiosities than for proper art. Small pieces of sculpture in bronze, lead and woods, a peculiar kind of abstrusely complicated table-center, clock and automaton, were particular favorites. Large sculpture in wood, like the agitated *Breisach Altar* (1526) by the Master H.L., developed in a manneristic Late Gothic of knobby character while the later secular bronze sculpture on façades and fountains followed Italian prototypes. Hubert Gerhard (1550-1620) spread the style of his teacher Giovanni da Bologna to southern Germany and the Dutch sculptor Adrien de Vries (1560-1627), who had the same training in Florence, modeled the emperor's *Bust* (Figure 12). He joined an international group of artists gathered in Prague to enliven with astonishing fancies and conceits the jaded and eccentric mind of the emperor. In this environment, Arcimboldo's contrived and ambiguous pictures, such as his *Allegories of the Four Elements* (Color slide 15), found their sophisticated appreciation. The emperor died insane after terrifying manias had overshadowed his late years. Soon France and Sweden emerged as new political powers and the collections in Prague were badly damaged and dispersed during the ravages of the Thirty Years' War.

During the Tudor era an increasing state absolutism and the rupture with Rome in 1531 left few challenging opportunities for painters in England; particularly religious frescoes and secular decorations remained scarce throughout the century. Portraits afforded practically the only source of steady income for the "needy artificers."

During the reign of Henry VIII more lavish and expansive building was undertaken, but after his death (1547), many foreign artists left England. His large palace *Nonsuch* was still a half-timbered structure with an odd mixture of Italianate and Late Gothic trimming. Later houses, *Longleat* (1567), *Hardwick Hall* (1576-97) and *Wollaton* (1580-88) all share a characteristic massing of cubes with large rectangular fenestration and increasing architectural ornamentation derived from Netherlandish scrollwork.

Sculpture was almost totally confined to architectural ornament and funerary monuments. But the highest standards for portrait painting had been set by the works of Hans Holbein the Younger (1497-1543) who first visited England in 1526-28 and returned there for good in 1532. Established as court painter to Henry VIII by 1536, he gave the lasting likenesses of the king, Jane Seymour, and many courtiers and prominent men. He also painted frescoes in Whitehall (now lost). His large double portrait of the French ambassadors to England (1533) may have helped him to secure a permanent position at the court (Figure 13). The many personal and elaborate allegorical allusions in this work liken it in concept to Bronzino's later *Portrait of Ugolino Martelli* (Color slide 7), but Holbein's dedicated descriptive rendering of things comes out of a long tradition in the North. Holbein's portraits remained the chief

model for English artists throughout the century, reinforced by the example of the Netherlandish painters Guillim Scrotes and Hans Eworth (active 1545-74) who succeeded Holbein as court painter and later worked for Queen Elizabeth.

Nicholas Hilliard (ca. 1547-1619) was the first English artist to grow to the stature of the foreigners. Trained as a goldsmith he painted only miniature portraits in watercolor on vellum in the luminous colors which book illuminators had been using for centuries (Color slide 16). Hilliard called himself an "imitator of Holbein's manner," but his linear, delicate style which pleased Queen Elizabeth, is in fact quite distinct from Holbein's, though it shares its elegance and refinement with French drawings and miniatures that Hilliard may have known before visiting France in 1576. Hilliard's pupil, Isaac Oliver, introduced Baroque practice in pose and particularly in the soft shading of colors, while Hilliard summed up his convictions and experiences in a treatise on *The Art of Limning* extolling the virtues of unshaded linear drawing "which showeth all to a good judgment."

English art of the sixteenth century remained certainly the least Italianate and in many ways the least varied. As a rule artists in Britain were not held in the same esteem as their colleagues on the continent and opportunities for important and independent work were very rare indeed.

Mannerist art in France is largely the product of Italian artists gathered at the court of Francis I in Fontainebleau. Contacts with Italy had been intense ever since the early sixteenth century when the campaigns of Louis XII and Francis I annexed Milan for a few years as a French colony. Elements of Italian Renaissance architecture made their appearance at *Blois* (1515-24) and *Chambord* (begun 1519), and Italian sculptors carved the tombs of the Duke of Orléans (1502) and of Louis XII (1515-31) at St. Denis.

Since his coronation Francis I systematically collected works by Italian masters through his agent Giovambattista della Palla and he encouraged Italian artists to come to France. Leonardo arrived in 1516; Sarto stayed a short time in 1518/19. In 1528 Francis decided to stabilize the court at Fontainebleau and put Gilles Le Breton in charge of the architectural improvements of an older hunting lodge there. An imposing gate and a long *Gallery* were added, for which the newly arrived Rosso Fiorentino (1530) and Francesco Primaticcio (1532) designed a highly original decoration combining a series of fourteen frescoes with surrounding sculpture and strap work in plaster (Color slide 17). Rosso was essentially responsible for the

paintings, the Bolognese Primaticcio most likely suggested, and certainly executed, the stucco-sculpture. Before coming to France he had been assisting Giulio Romano in Mantua on just this kind of decoration. But Rosso and Primaticcio did much more than merely repeat Italian work in France. The gallery of Francis I introduces a kind of stucco decoration which spread rapidly to surrounding countries.

In the year of Rosso's death, 1540, Cellini arrived in Fontainebleau; Vignola and Serlio followed a year later. Serlio (1475-1554) spent the rest of his life in France building very little but exercising a decisive influence on architectural design and practice through his writings. Cellini left an impressive example of his bronze sculpture with the *Nymph of Fountainebleau* and startled the king with a precious work of inventive design, the *Saltcellar of Francis I* (1540-43).

Among contemporary French artists the sculptor Jean Goujon (died ca. 1567) formulated his own relief style blending a refined classicism with the elegant and antagonistic poses of Primaticcio's. A series of shallow bas-reliefs from the *Fountain of the Innocents* (1547-49) in Paris can also in part be related to works by Rosso and his collaborators (Figure 14). Germain Pilon (ca. 1535-90) overshadows Goujon with his monumental *Tomb of Henry II and Catherine de'Medici* (1563-70) in which he successfully fused the French tradition of Gothic tombs with vigorous sculpture in marble and bronze that owes to Italian models almost as much as it does to Burgundian prototypes.

Very little is known of the painter Jean (or Janet) Clouet (died ca. 1540) who had probably come from Brussels. His work approximates Italian and French traditions while his son François (died 1572) — succeeding him as court painter in 1541 — renewed the Italian strain particularly in portraiture. Examples of Salviati's and Bronzino's work, like the *Allegory* now in London, were collected by Francis I and may very likely have acquainted François Clouet with the more recent tendencies of Italian Mannerism. Rosso's death in 1540 left a gap which French painters were hardly able to fill, a reason Primaticcio himself advanced for inviting Niccolò dell'Abate (ca. 1512-71) to Fontainebleau. Niccolò's training in Modena and Bologna and his familiarity with Upper Italian and Venetian painting—particularly that of Dosso—introduced a new kind of fantastic landscape painting at Fontainebleau where he soon absorbed the cooler tones of the Antwerp Mannerists (Color slide 18). In 1559, a Frenchman, Antoine Caron, was made court painter by Catherine de'Medici, wife of Henry II. Caron (ca. 1525-1600) painted larger pictures with ambitious historical subjects, courtly ceremonies and allegories usually setting up a vast architectural "stage" in which many small and gracefully agitating figures create an impression of aimless and incessant movement.

One theme, and its endless variations, dominates the School of Fontainebleau: courtly love in mythological guise. A precious eroticism pervades the many portraits of courtesans and ladies at their toilets (Color slide 19) and at levées, and their playful masquerading as Diana, Venus and Nymph.

With the death of Primaticcio in 1570 and of Niccolò dell' Abate in 1571, the so-called *First School of Fontainebleau* came to a close. The last quarter of the century was dominated by French, and increasingly by Netherlandish, painters who were less and less sensitive to the works of Rosso, Primaticcio and Niccolò dell'Abate without however being able to create an art comparable in quality to that of the Italian immigrants.

Fontainebleau was the first court north of the Alps to throw its doors wide open to Italian Mannerism. But more than merely turning it into a scion of Italian art, Rosso, Primaticcio and Niccolò dell'Abate formulated a courtly style at Fontainebleau which is neither paralleled in Italy nor contained in their own earlier works. Soon French artists, like the architects Philibert de L'Orme (ca. 1510-70) and Lescot (1500/15-1578)

Figure 14. Jean Goujon: Nymph from the "Fountain of the Innocents". Louvre, Paris

with whom Goujon collaborated, and the painters Jean Cousin the Elder, Jean and François Clouet and Caron, recast their Italian lessons in an idiom of their own. Their work is distinguished by a preference for cool, enamel-like colors, and a taste for the precious. Though a bit affected and rhetorical at times, their paintings never lack subtlety and elegance.

During the fifteenth and early sixteenth centuries the Netherlands were recognized as the center of Northern Renaissance art. After 1500 painters like Quentin Massys, Jan van Scorel and Joos van Cleve sustained this tradition, but Italian Mannerism made itself felt early and strongly. Pieter Bruegel the Elder — the greatest Netherlandish painter of his century — stands apart from the many imitators of Italian Mannerism, defining a stylistic sphere of his own. Yet his art shares more with Mannerism than with any other major aspect of sixteenth-century painting. Bruegel's moralizing and often symbolic use of "low" subjects from peasant life and his pictures of tales and proverbs follow the Mannerist compulsion to stretch images into verbal and allegorical concepts.

Throughout the sixteenth century the Netherlands were torn by religious strife and political struggle for independence, until the northern provinces united in the seventies and emerged as an independent republic. The southern provinces (today Belgium) remained under Spanish domination.

During the reign of Charles V (1519-56) Antwerp rose to unprecedented commercial power; here goods from central Europe and England were exchanged in the lucrative Portuguese spice trade. The city also leaped to artistic prominence with Mabuse, Bruegel, Frans Floris and a whole school of painters called the Antwerp Mannerists.

Quenten Massys (1464/6-1530) who began as a follower of Jan van Eyck tried to emulate the *sfumato* and the physiognomical variety of Leonardo's work. Significantly, the younger

Antwerp painter Jan Gossaert, called Mabuse (died ca. 1535), wished to deepen his knowledge of Italian art. Reaching Rome in 1508 in the retinue of Philip of Burgundy, he copied extensively antique works and experienced the overpowering impact of Italian Renaissance art. No work is known of the first years after his return from Italy, but by 1515/16 his large pictures of nude figures (*Adam and Eve*) drew on Dürer as well as on Italian art. They fuse the cold colors and meticulous detail of earlier Netherlandish painting with Mabuse's more grandiose intentions stimulated in Italy. Mabuse introduced mythological nudity in the Netherlands, with his life size *Hercules and Amphitrite* (1516) painted for his patron Philip of Burgundy, and with delightful cabinet pieces like *Venus and Cupid* of 1521 (Color slide 20).

Joachim Patinier (ca. 1480-1524) specialized in small landscape paintings built up in panoramic horizontal stripes receding over fantastic rock formations into the cold blue distance.

When Raphael's tapestries for the Sistine Chapel were woven in Brussels between 1516 and 1519, their impact made new converts to Italianate art. Bernaert van Orley, Mabuse and his pupil Jan van Scorel (1495-1562) and other artists in Antwerp shared in the effort of absorbing Italian lessons into their own idiom. Trips to Rome became more and more imperative and Scorel, as well as his pupil Maerten van Heemskerck (1498-1574), spent considerable time there busily catching up with Italian developments. But when Pieter Bruegel the Elder (ca. 1525/30-1569) traveled across the Alps to the Holy City in 1552/53, he seemed to have had eyes only for majestic alpine landscape. Many of his landscapes and genre scenes were engraved in the shop of Hieronymus Cock for whom he also drew more recondite religious parables in the manner of Bosch. Few pictures are known from the fifties, but before moving to Brussels around 1563, he had painted his *Proverbs, Children's Games* and the large Bosch-like *Triumph of Death*. All of these

Figure 15. Bruegel:
The Parable of the Blind.
Museo Nazionale, Naples

depend for their understanding on the interchange between
verbal and pictorial concepts, but during his years in Brussels,
Bruegel developed increasingly subtle and pictorially novel
means. His scenes of peasant life were, of course, not intended
for rural people but were appreciated and collected by King
Philip II, the Emperor Rudolph II and learned patrons like the
diplomat, Cardinal Granvella. *The Parable of the Blind* of 1568
(Figure 15) typifies Bruegel's capacity to constitute metaphorical meaning even in a candidly observed reality. Painted in
matte, sandy tempera, the *Parable* renders a group of blind
beggars stumbling along a precariously sloping path. As the first
falls into a ditch their expressions change from numbness and

bewilderment to horror. But this is more than an unfortunate accident. A church in the quiet countryside emphasizes the religious significance of Christ's parable on the Pharisees: "And if the blind lead the blind, both shall fall into the ditch" (*Matthew, XV, 12-14*). Blindness remains only superficially a physical handicap, it is also a metaphor for the error and delusion of those who cannot see the divine light. Through their baleful appearance in a peaceful landscape, the blind convey the universal image of the blindness of fate and the inescapable danger of stumbling and falling on the path of one's life which leads through a world of dry and drab colors. Not unlike Albrecht Altdorfer (Color slide 13), Bruegel likes to dwarf man and his activities in vast landscapes beautifully attuned to the changing moods of day and season. In his *Tower of Babel* (Color slide 21) the viewer embraces a wide landscape out of which the hybrid structure grows into the clouds, very much as Jan van Eyck left the rising tower of a cathedral in an unfinished picture (Antwerp) of 1437. Certainly Bruegel's minute detail owes much to the tradition of Netherlandish painting, and yet his inexhaustable inventiveness creates less of a world in which God inhabits every detail, than it engulfs man's work and life in a void through which they appear gratuitous and tragic. The fresco of the *Conversion of Paul* (Color slide 8) in the Pauline Chapel makes strikingly clear how Michelangelo transformed his heroic figures into vessels of an inward event, while Bruegel (Color slide 22) makes the miracle occur in an indifferent world of overwhelming vastness. Bruegel's work is unique. His independence from Italy, his penetrating vision and choice of subject rendered in complex pictorial terms make him one of the most original painters of the sixteenth century.

Bruegel's son, Pieter (1564-1638), copied many of his father's famous works, and his second son, Jan (1568-1625), became a still-life painter and later collaborated with Rubens. Still-lifes were among the favorite Netherlandish paintings of the seventeenth century, but like pure landscapes (Lucas van Valkenborch; Gillis van Conixloo, Paul Bril), they had already originated in the sixteenth century when painters like Pieter Aertsen (1509-1575) painted kitchens and vendors' displays on almost life-size scale. Usually these still lifes imply an allegorical meaning or, as in the case of Aertsen's *Meat Stall* (Figure 16), include a religious reference in the background where the Flight into Egypt contrasts with the crude display of meat.

During the last years of Bruegel's life, religious wars flared up and soon many artists fled the Netherlands when iconoclasts destroyed their works or the Catholic inquisition threatened to reprimand them. At the turn of the century Rubens traveled to Italy but followed neither the "Romanist's" subjugation under Italian art nor Bruegel's disregard of it.

Since the fifteenth century, Netherlandish art was collected in Spain and northern artists worked there long before Spaniards traveled to Italy and began to follow Italian models. Spanish art of the sixteenth century remained almost exclusively ecclesiastical. The country of Ignatius of Loyola, Teresa of Avila and Saint John of the Cross, the center of imperial counter-reformatory politics and of inquisition, not only conceived of state and religion in the same terms, it also attracted the most ecstatically religious painter, El Greco, and its colonists and priests carried this art into the Americas and other dominions.

Several Spanish artists like Machuca, Alonso Berruguete and Diego da Siloe had a first-hand acquaintance with Italian Renaissance and Early Mannerist art. Alonso Berruguete (ca. 1488-1561), the son of Pedro, not only absorbed Italian lessons during his stay in Florence (ca. 1504-1517) but may have played a considerable role in the formation of early Florentine Mannerism. His sculptural work at Valladolid and Toledo exaggerates intricate poses from Leonardo's drawings and Michelangelo's sculpture in an inner drama of religious experience.

Figure 16.   Pieter Aertsen:
The Meat Stall.
Museum, Uppsala University,
Uppsala, Sweden

Anguished facial expressions link even his later Spanish work with Rosso's and Pontormo's Florentine paintings.

Valencia was particularly open to Italian art: either Ferrando de Llanos or Ferrando Yáñez is the artist referred to as "ferrando spagnuolo" who assisted Leonardo in Florence in 1505. Vincente Juan Macip (ca. 1475-1545) and his son Juan de Juanes (ca. 1523-79) followed Italian examples with their religious paintings. Leonardo's *sfumato*, gracefully intricate poses and other more modish attributes of later Italian painting, were eagerly incorporated into their altarpieces, but the most accomplished among native painters is Luis de Morales (ca. 1520/25-86) from Estremadura. He was probably trained in a shop where Netherlandish painting was closely followed but soon his interest turned to works by Leonardo and his Milanese and Spanish imitators. Darkly veiled tones, the somber glow of colors and an affected expressiveness in gestures and facial features characterize his many Holy Families (Color slide 23) and altarpieces.

Charles V, who abdicated in 1556 in favor of his brother Ferdinand I and of his son Philip II, tended more and more toward Spain. He commissioned a Palace at Granada, which was begun in 1527, after plans by Machuca. Machuca had been working in Italy, and at Granada he fully displayed his command of Italian Renaissance architecture which was already slanting towards a less orthodox handling of familiar elements. Philip II called on another Spaniard with experience in Italy when he charged Juan Bautista de Toledo with the planning of the Escorial in 1559. Palace, monastery and a mausoleum for Charles V were to be combined in this vast structure of coldly geometricized design, into which only Juan de Herrera (ca. 1530-97) brought some relief, though he also planned the equally austere church of vast proportions.

Charles V had appointed Titian as his official portrait painter and knighted him in 1533. When the immense structure of the Escorial required decorations, Titian was the obvious choice. But he declined, as did his fellow-Venetian Tintoretto. In 1583 Luca Cambiaso (Color slide 3) traveled to Spain where he spent the last two years of his life. Federico Zuccaro followed in 1585 but left in 1588 when the king was disenchanted with his frescoes. In the same year, the Milanese Pelegrino Tibaldi (1527-96) arrived at the Escorial and, assisted by his shop, frescoed the library and the large cloister in a rather rhetorical manner derived from Michelangelo's late works. The entire decorations of the Escorial are, however, far below what Philip could have gotten from a man painting in a somber studio at Toledo. El Greco, recorded in Toledo in 1577, executed the High Altar for the church of San Domingo al Antiguo (1579)

Figure 17.   El Greco:
Christ at Gethsemane.
Toledo Museum of Art, Gift
of Edward Drummond Libbey

thus introducing the Venetian polyptych to Spain. El Greco hoped to gain Philip's favor with a small panel of the *Adoration of the Holy Name of Jesus.* A large version was ordered from El Greco and another picture commissioned with the *Martyrdom of St. Maurice and the Theban Legion.* In this visionary work — recalling Pontormo's fragmented settings and the feverish brushwork and color of Tintoretto — El Greco achieved the fervent intensity of an hallucination. But Philip's taste had been fed on Titian, and a short letter from the king's secretary refused acceptance of El Greco's work. Henceforward El Greco painted in Toledo for churches and convents developing his uncompromising visionary art which fuses heaven and earth (Figure 17). Two *Views of Toledo* and the very late *Laocoön* (Color slide 24) are his only non-devotional works, but they are permeated by the same spiritual drama as his religious paintings. In many ways El Greco has been considered the arch-mannerist in his complete subjugation of matter and color to the fervent demands of his immaterial vision.

The history of the arts in the sixteenth century is marked not only by a greater mobility of artists and an often rapid exchange of ideas, but also by the decisive and lasting consequences of traveling artists. Roger van der Weyden's trip to Italy in 1450 left few discernable traces in his own or in Italian art, but Dürer's and Mabuse's experiences there had a far-reaching effect on the further Italianization of the North, while Dürer's impact on some Italian painters had almost equal force. During the later sixteenth century, the Flemish sculptor Giovanni da Bologna dominated in Upper Italy, where he trained the Dutchman Adrien de Vries who later worked in Germany and finally moved to Prague. A new type of migrant artist appeared in the many Italians who spent most of their artistic careers in courtly centers of the North and the group of Northerners who often successfully sought their fortune in Italy. The international character of much later sixteenth-century art is a result of continental, rather than strictly local or national, awareness in aristocratic centers under the consolidated empire. The scale of the world jumped to global proportions after Magellan's expedition in 1522 and the conquest of vast new territories.

In 1543 Copernicus published his new theory of a heliocentric universe and Vesalius offered, in the same year, the first scientific anatomy of the human body, both supporting their theories by observation and experiments rather than authorization quotations only. The new theory of the universe saw the earth among the planets moving through the vast and dark expanses of an infinite sky — at once an image for the lone and gratuitous place of man whose fate seemed prone to fall from God's grace at any moment. Mannerist painters from Pontormo to El Greco were able to render everything they touched metaphoric of this spiritual precariousness of human life. Others, like Giulio Romano or Arcimboldo, expressed more frivolously their debunking or highly contrived awareness that firm ground and pre-established harmony were thoroughly lacking.

· 1 ·

ROSSO FIORENTINO
(1495-1540)
Deposition
(1521)
Panel, 11′ x 6′ 5½″
Pinacoteca, Volterra

Rosso Fiorentino, a colleague of Pontormo in the Sarto shop, made his debut as an independent artist with the fresco of the *Assumption of Mary* (1516) in the atrium of the Santissima Annunziata where Sarto, Franciabigio and Pontormo all worked side by side during the 1510's. Though the unruly style of the young Rosso is plainly evident in the *Assumption*, his *Deposition* of 1521 in Volterra marks a violent break with High Renaissance concepts. Rosso must have known the *Deposition* (Uffizi) which Perugino finished for Filippino Lippi early in the century, but this dependence is almost obliterated by a new violence in color and brushwork. Overlapping silhouettes cut every obvious link to the earlier work, especially among the men struggling to lower the effeminate, livid body of Christ from the cross. The figures are grouped more in terms of surface patterns than as fully rounded bodies. Anxiety marks their faces and seems to contort every outline. Broad cross-hatching and deliberately rough brush strokes give a sketchy quality to the upper areas of the painting where haggard faces and impetuous gestures contrast with the contained and grief-stricken figures of the Marys and Saint John below. The ladders and the cross stand out against the icy, pre-dawn sky while the colors of the garments glow in harshly modeled reds and yellows. In contrast to the High Renaissance gradation of tones, Rosso's jagged shapes of harsh colors and aggressively outlined silhouettes are typically Mannerist. Much like Pontormo's *Joseph in Egypt* (National Gallery, London), Rosso's *Deposition* was commissioned for an unspectacular place, but nonetheless it set a decisive and influential example of the new art striving for expressive qualities rather than self-contained balance.

**DOMENICO
BECCAFUMI**
(1485/6-1551)
Birth of the Virgin
1544
Panel,
Pinacoteca, Siena

Domenico Beccafumi, called Mecuccio or Mecarino, went to Rome in 1510 and returned to his native Siena in 1512 as one of the few Tuscan artists with a first-hand knowledge of Roman High Renaissance art. In provincial Siena he began working on frescoes in the hospital of Santa Maria della Scala. Later, he decorated a large ceiling in the town hall with allegorical figures and events from ancient history (1529-35), introducing steeply foreshortened views. Beccafumi was also active in Genoa and after his return in 1542 continued to design scenes from the Old Testament for the marble inlay of the Cathedral floor.

The *Birth of the Virgin* of 1544 was painted for the nuns of San Paolo when Beccafumi had long established himself in Siena as a painter of eccentric large altarpieces, like the terrifying vision of the inferno in his *Last Judgment* (Pinacoteca, Siena). In the *Birth of the Virgin* Beccafumi's waxen colors, melting under an irrationally directed light, and the strangely isolated figures create a haunted atmosphere. The transparent colors and their luminous shot-effect are often comparable to Pontormo's earlier work (Color slide 6).

· 3 ·

LUCA CAMBIASO
(1527-1585)
Christ before Caiaphas
Canvas, 74″ x 54½″
Palazzo Bianco, Genoa

Luca Cambiaso studied the frescoes in Genoese palaces painted by Perino del Vaga and Pordenone, and soon assisted his father in this kind of decoration. Exposed to Northern Italian work, particularly by Correggio, Cambiaso evolved a strikingly novel style for a series of night pieces, in which the flicker of candles and reflected light along with the close-up view seem to point towards Caravaggio's work after 1600 and to that of Northern painters like Georges de La Tour.

Through his collaboration with the Bergamesque architect, sculptor, and painter Giambattista Castello, Luca may also have intensified his contact with Venetian painting. In the year of the Jubilee, 1575, he traveled to Rome via Florence, and then in 1583 went to Spain (where Castello had gone in 1567) and spent the last two years of his life frescoing the vault above the main altar in the church of the Escorial.

The tenebrism (low-keyed dark colors) of Luca's *Christ before Caiaphas* is shared by a *Madonna* (Palazzo Bianco, Genoa) and several *Adorations* (in private collections) for which a date in the 1570's appears most likely. The unusually dramatic character of these night pieces is heightened in the scene of Christ before the High Priest, as the reverberating light of candles nervously silhouettes bodies and faces against the dark background. The almost life-size figures in *Christ before Caiaphas* help to focus on the confrontation between the rugged face of the High Priest, the grimacing soldiers and the fragile profile of Christ. The staging of the scene and its dramatic lighting draw the viewer into the circle of witnesses around the central group.

· 4 ·

FRANCESCO PARMIGIANINO
(1503-1540)

Madonna with St. Zachary, the Magdalen and St. John

Panel, 28½″ x 24½″
Uffizi, Florence

With his *Self-Portrait* (Figure 4) the young Parmigianino gave a striking example of his eccentric and elegant style when he was about twenty years old. His stay in Rome (from which he barely escaped during the sack of 1527) and his study of early Mannerist painting by pupils of Raphael, are echoed in his *Madonna with St. Zachary* along with reminiscences of Correggio's grace.

Before settling again in his home town of Parma, Parmigianino worked for a short time in Bologna and there delivered this painting to Bonifazio Gozzadini in 1530. However, he had to keep pressing him for payment repeatedly over the next years. Less extravagant than the contemporary *Saint Rocchus* (San Petronio, Bologna), and less ambitious than the well-known *Madonna with the Long Neck* of 1535 (Uffizi), this *Madonna* reveals Parmigianino's distinctive elegance and refinement of features and gestures. Between the classicizing profile of the Magdalen in the upper left and the closer profile of Zachary in the lower right, a sequence of shifting diagonals govern the Madonna and the children while securing a dominant central position for the Virgin. The loosely brushed autumn colors, heightened with blue and purple in rather sudden gradation, contribute to the "discordant harmonies" of an unsuspected pictorial complexity. The Arch of Constantine and a Roman column in the background are souvenirs of Parmigianino's recent stay in Rome, poetically translated into a fantastic landscape almost in the manner of Giulio Romano. Despite early death, preceded by sad years of melancholy isolation and agonizing work on his frescoes in Santa Maria della Stecchata at Parma, Parmigianino, together with Giulio, helped disseminate Roman Mannerism in upper Italy.

· 5 ·

GIULIO ROMANO
(ca. 1499-1546)
The Fall of the Giants
Fresco
Palazzo del Te, Mantua

The construction of the Palazzo del Te, a suburban villa for Federico II Gonzaga, was begun in 1525 by Giulio Romano who completed the interior decorations in stucco and fresco ten years later. The decorations of an extraordinary room in the southeastern corner of the main building quadrangle, the *Sala dei Giganti* (Room of the Giants), date from the last years of the campaign. The local painter Rinaldo Mantovano executed the frescoes after Giulio's cartoons.

Close in size to Raphael's *stanze* in the Vatican (where Giulio was his main assistant), the *Room of the Giants* makes a most striking contrast to the dignified equilibrium of the *Stanza della Segnatura*, for example. Giulio vaulted the *Room of the Giants* on the principle of an oven, excluding any painted or actual architectural members. The Olympian deities appear on a ring of clouds and Jupiter smashes with his thunderbolts — an emblem of the Gonzagas — the brute race of the giants. Storms, earthquakes and floods are unleashed to bury the giants under collapsing buildings and in volcanic craters. The mosaic on the floor simulates the pattern of concentric waves, the vault throws back a gruesome echo, and at night the flicker of the fireplace and of candles transformed the room into a chamber "awakening fear and horror," as Vasari describes it.

· 6 ·

JACOPO
DA PONTORMO
(1494-1556)
Deposition
(1526-1528)
Panel, 123″ x 75½″
Santa Felicità, Florence

In 1525 Lodovico Capponi commissioned Pontormo to decorate a small chapel in the church of San Felicità. The frescoes in the vault are now destroyed, but four roundels with the *Evangelists* and a fresco of the *Annunciation* are still in place together with the large *Deposition*. In the years before 1525, Pontormo had monumentalized the Lord's Passion in an astounding fresco cycle at the Certosa (near Florence), and his *Deposition* is still imbued with the same intensity acquired through a productive dialogue with Dürer's woodcuts of the *Passion*. Rather than conforming to any one of the standard types of Deposition, Deploration or Entombment, Pontormo presents the dead Saviour and the group of mourners for devout and mystical contemplation. Perugino, Fra Bartolommeo and Pontormo's former teacher Andrea del Sarto, had painted large *Deplorations of Christ*, but Raphael departed from earlier Florentine types with his *Entombment* (Galleria Borghese, Rome) of 1507. Pontormo not only rendered the event in much more inward terms, he was also able to give it a visionary quality through the cool and yet sharply pitched colors. The grieving Marys and the group of mourners seem to gyrate around a bluish sphere in the center of the picture. All external elements are either removed, or completely attuned (like the cloud in the upper left) to the inward experience of the tragic event. Even the tulip colors ranging from icy blue to flaming red have a luminescence symbolic of the pictorial meaning. Pontormo's *Deposition* is probably the most beautiful and accomplished work of Florentine Mannerism and one of the high points in Pontormo's unique *oeuvre*.

· 7 ·

AGNOLO BRONZINO
(1503-1572)

Portrait of Ugolino Martelli
(c. 1539)
Panel, 40" x 33"
State Museums, Berlin

After initial training by Raffaellino del Garbo, Bronzino became a pupil of Pontormo and remained his life-long friend and admirer. Bronzino's portrait painting matured after 1530 and with its air of detachment, officiality and cold elegance, was ideally suited for the court of Cosimo I.

Shortly before 1540, Bronzino painted the young Ugolino Martelli who later became bishop of Grandèves in Southern France. The youth is seated in the courtyard of the family *palazzo* in Florence. Through posture and various objects, a number of personal and rather recondite allusions are made: Ugolino's pose recalls Michelangelo's statue of Giuliano de'Medici (Medici Chapel); in the background Donatello's *David of the Casa Martelli* (now in the National Gallery, Washington, D. C.) is erected on a sixteenth-century pedestal; Ugolino's right hand points to the opening lines of the ninth Canto in Homer's *Iliad* lying on a small table side by side with another volume lettered MARO (Virgil Maro); his left arm rests on a volume of Bembo, the Venetian historian and man of letters with whom Ugolino later corresponded. There may be a parallel suggested between David's couragous victory over Goliath and Achilles' admonishing of the weary Greeks before Troy; as well as a comparison between Virgil's and Bembo's accomplishments in the Latin and Italian tongues. The complex architectural setting interacts with the turning and torsion of the sitter and emphasizes Bronzino's indirect characterization of the subjects of his portraits.

· 8 ·

MICHELANGELO
(1475-1564)

Conversion of Paul
(1543/44)
Fresco
Pauline Chapel, Vatican, Rome

Michelangelo received the commission for the frescoes in the Pauline Chapel shortly before the completion of the *Last Judgment*. He probably finished the *Conversion of Paul* by 1543/44, and began the companion fresco only in 1546. The contemporary theorist, Lomazzo, recognized here the inception of Michelangelo's style of his old age. In a highly unusual way Michelangelo juxtaposed the *Conversion of Paul* with the *Crucifixion of Peter*, each time rendering the event with a novel appeal to the beholder. The most decisive traits of these frescoes in the Pope's chapel are a new concept of dramatic narration and a dominance of sign-like, abstract patterns. A strong parabolic movement governs the *Conversion*, as a shaft of light emerges from the arm of Christ, blinds the fallen Paul and, through the standing figure at the right, returns heavenwards where angels appear in the upper right.

In a barren landscape near Damascus, Paul's train disperses in fright and his horse shies towards the rear as the miraculous conversion literally evacuates the place and paralyzes the fallen body of Paul. Antique sources were used for the figure of Paul as well as for the grouping of horse and groom, but Michelangelo employed them fully to his own purposes. The profound religious symbols which Michelangelo infused into his Pauline frescoes have been convincingly related to the reform movement of the *Spirituali* transmitted to Michelangelo mainly through Vittoria Colonna, his friend who died when he was in the midst of working on the chapel.

39

9

JACOPO TINTORETTO
(1518-1594)

*The Discovery of the
Body of St. Mark*
(1562-66)

Canvas, 161″ x 161″
Brera, Milan

After training and association with one of the Bordone and with Schia-vone, Tintoretto was made a master in 1539. But only after the forties do we have a clear idea about his work. Tintoretto's early paintings betray his interest in Parmigianino and demonstrate his capacity to draw suc-cessfully from various sources. His large canvas with *St. Mark Rescuing a Slave* (Accademia, Venice) made him instantly famous in 1548. The more decorative qualities of his earlier paintings had given way to a dramatically focused scene which uses boldly foreshortened views and in-tense colors to control masses of figures.

The *Discovery of the Body of St. Mark* (1562-66) belongs in a group of three canvases. Here Tintoretto creates a steeply funneled setting in which the Venetians frantically search sarcophagi in Constantinople for the body of their patron saint who miraculously appears on the left un-der raking light. The repetition of identical bays and floor-tiles into depth is given a hypnotic appearance in the flickering reflections of torchlight. The overscaled decrease, from the huge foreground figures to the body-less shadows moving in the rear, emphasizes the diagonal pull and ten-sion of the composition. Tintoretto's rapid brush is already dissolving every solid object in the nervous strokes of its dryly applied color. Highly theatrical in its narration the *Discovery of the Body of St. Mark* also opens a new phase in Tintoretto's search for an emotional fusion of bodies and colors.

10

JACOPO TINTORETTO
(1518-1594)

Ascension of Christ

Canvas, 211½″ x 127½″
Scuola di San Rocco, Venice

With his grand cycles of the *Life of Christ* (late 1560's) and of *Mary* (1582-87) in the halls of the Confraternity of Saint Roch (Scuola di San Rocco) Tintoretto enlarges his earlier brushwork to the scale of gestures. Tintoretto's contact with this brotherhood goes back to 1549, but only in 1565 did he become a member and was then contracted to decorate their building. The *Ascension of Christ*, from the cycle of the upper hall, com-pletely dissolves the picture field into a cloud-like array of ovoid shapes rising above the tilted ground behind a *repoussoir* figure on the left. Emphatic gestures, an almost transparent application of paint in agitated broad strokes, and the burning intensity of his deep colors make the late canvasses at the Scuola di San Rocco comparable only to the visionary dematerialization of form and color in the later work of El Greco.

Tintoretto's two sons and his daughter contributed, among others, to the large shop work of his late years. The fires in the Doges' Palace in 1574 and 1577 necessitated new decorations which Tintoretto shared with his contemporary, Paolo Veronese (ca. 1528-88).

· 11 ·

TITIAN

(ca. 1480s-1576)

Pietà

Canvas, 138″ x 155½″
Accademia, Venice

Titian's longevity links the early High Renaissance in Venice — when he collaborated with Giorgione — to the mature phases of Tintoretto's dramatic paintings in the Scuola di San Rocco. The *Pietà* is among the last pictures on which Titian had worked leaving it not quite completed at his death in 1576. His pupil Palma Giovane put in the finishing touches and then presented the large canvas to the church of Sant'Angelo, recounting the history of this work in the Latin inscription at the bottom.

The niche in Mannerist *rustica* is flanked by the statues of Moses on the left and of the Hellespontian Sibyl on the right. A small votive-panel on the right pedestal shows Titian and his son Orazio prostrated in prayer. The asymmetrical triangle of the central group with the Pietà is complemented by the anguished Magdalen stepping forward on the left and Joseph of Arimathaea — or more likely St. Jerome — kneeling on the right. While St. Jerome, Mary and Magdalen are pictorially united in an ascending diagonal towards the left, the body of Christ is counterpoised alone towards the upper right where — after an interval in the gloomy void of the niche — a flying putto wields a torch, referring to the resurrection of the Saviour despite his bodily death. This beautiful work is saturated with Titian's unique capacity to shape figures in terms of color alone, (the grieving group and the oppressive architecture — related to that of Giulio Romano) set in a gloom of somber hues, which nevertheless glow almost with the intensity of stained glass.

· 12 ·

GRUNEWALD

(Mathias Gothardt)

(ca. 1470-1528)

Resurrection of Christ
from the Isenheim Altar

Panel, 8′ 10″ x 4′ 8¼″
Museum Unterlinden, Colmar

The Antonine house of Isenheim was under the priorate of Guido Ghersi, a Sicilian (died 1516), when Grünewald received the commission for a large new altarpiece. With its two pairs of movable wings, the Isenheim altar belongs to a distinctly Northern type of which van Eyck and Pacher had given impressive examples. The Isenheim altar has three "phases": on the closed shutters, the large Crucifixion is flanked by St. Anthony Abbot and St. Sebastian; after the first opening, *Mary in the Temple* occupies the central area and the *Annunciation* and the *Resurrection* span God's incarnation in the flesh; the third stage opposes *St. Anthony and St. Paul* in devout conversation, to the *Temptation of St. Anthony* with its ghastly monsters recalling Schongauer and Bosch, while the center is occupied by a sculpted group by Nikolaus Hagenauer.

Completed before Ghersi's death, the Isenheim altar contains many allusions to St. Anthony's fire — a widespread, dreadful disease of that time caused by ergot — for the cure of which the Antonine order had established many hospitals.

The tall panel with the *Resurrection of Christ* expresses in mystical terms of light and color a theme often depicted by Northern artists of the time. Christ ascends to heaven in a sphere of supernatural light almost dissolving in sheer glow the figure of the Lord. The sleeping soldiers at the tomb are paralyzed under the impact of the miraculous event, as Christ surges upwards, his shroud floating loose in rainbow colors.

ALBRECHT
ALTDORFER
(ca. 1480-1538)
*Battle of Alexander
and Darius (detail)*
(1529)
Panel, 62″ x 47″
Alte Pinakothek, Munich

A native of Bavaria, Altdorfer spent most of his life in Regensburg where he served as a town-counsellor and held the post of city architect by 1526. In 1528 Duke Wilhelm IV of Bavaria ordered a set of historic battle pieces for the decoration of a room in his new residence in Munich. Eight panels (Alte Pinakothek, Munich and National Museum, Stockholm) survive, but none compares favorably with Altdorfer's *Battle of Alexander* (1529).

The epochal encounter between Alexander and the gigantic Persian army at Issus was known in detail through the colorful account of the Roman historian Curtius. The specific program of Duke Wilhelm's cycle of battle pieces may have been drawn up by his court historian Aventin (1477-1534).

Altdorfer staged the battle in a wide river bed between steep mountain ranges under a vast sky with the sun eclipsing the moon. The armies are almost contemporary in dress, and banners listing the men and losses on both sides show that certain historical documents were consulted. Turkish elements in dress and pomp give further hints of the contemporary identification of the Persians with the Turks of the Ottoman Empire of Altdorfer's day.

Pictorially Altdorfer developed his painting from records of contemporary wars, such as the exploits of Maximilian which were chronicled in illuminated manuscripts. There remains in Altdorfer's work an element of these miniatures as well as a specifically Northern insistence upon narrative detail. In the midst of clashing armies the two kings are drawing towards each other as in a chivalric ballad. The wide landscape, extending to the curved horizon, affords a view in depth and width which anticipates Bruegel's late work (Color slides 21, 22). The distance from the historic event enlarges the beholder's view to universal proportions as moon and sun, night and day, tune into human history.

**LUCAS CRANACH
THE ELDER**
(1472-1553)
Apollo and Diana
(1530)
Panel, 18½″ x 13¾″
State Museums, Berlin

A contemporary of Dürer and Grünewald, Lucas Cranach the Elder served three electors of Saxony from 1505 to his death. The son of a painter, his two sons grew up to become painters as well, with Lucas the Younger (1515-1586) carrying on his father's manner.

Lucas the Elder is particularly important for the early years of the so-called "Danube School." His portraits of the Viennese humanist *Johannes Cuspinian and his Wife* (Private Collection, Switzerland) of 1502/3 and his *Crucifixion* (Munich) of 1503 are of youthful boldness and freedom, achieved by swirling brushwork and highly expressive coloration. Since his stay in Vienna (ca. 1500-1504), Cranach excelled in portraits and imaginative landscape backgrounds for his religious and mythological paintings. In 1505 the elector Frederick the Wise called Cranach to Wittenberg where he met Luther, symphathized with the reformer and supported him with woodcuts and pamphlets printed in his prosperous shop.

Cranach's erotic mythologies were in great demand (and hence exist in numerous versions): the *Judgment of Paris* and *Venus and Cupid* are set in elaborately enmeshed landscapes or contrast delicate flesh tones with a dark background.

Signed and dated 1530, *Apollo and Diana* exemplifies Cranach's blend of Northern descriptive and anecdotal detail with the theme of mythological nudity indirectly derived from Italy. Cranach's sources are quite complex: his brushwork is indebted to Dürer, as is, more specifically, the standing figure of Apollo, but Diana has been posed in the manner of the famous antique sculpture of a boy pulling a thorn from his foot. The often deliberately erotic poses of Cranach's modish beauties set a tone which was exploited more boldly by the fashionable painters at the court of Emperor Rudolph II in Prague.

· 15 ·

GIUSEPPE
ARCIMBOLDO
(1527-1593)

Allegory of Fire
(1566)

Panel, 26″ x 20″
Kunsthistorisches Museum,
Vienna

The Milanese Arcimboldo became court painter to Ferdinand I in 1562, remaining in Prague under Maximilian II and Rudolph II until 1587 when he retired to his native city and was elevated to Count Palatine. For his patron Maximilian II, Arcimboldo conceived a series of *Four Elements* of which two survive; *Fire* and *Water* (1566). Three years earlier he had painted similar allegories of the *Four Seasons*. The *Fire*, signed and dated 1566, is the most spectacular of Arcimboldo's conceits. A personification of Fire has been assembled from various pistols, candles, canons, lamps and live coal painted in trompe-l'oeil detail. Visual and mental image are fused in a typical conceit as all the objects are directly used to strike fire, and at the same time, so composed as to form an allegorical personification of that element. Ranging from sandy browns to the golden yellow of bees-wax, from the luster of bronze to the blaze of fire in the tufts of hair, Arcimboldo succeeds not only in his concept but also as a painter. To increase the shine he applied gold-leaf before painting in the burning coal, again ambiguously confounding painted glimmer and actual reflection of light.

Arcimboldo was famous with his contemporaries for the design and direction of elaborate festivities at the imperial court, and for his experiments to correlate sounds and colors. But above all he was known for his intriguing pictorial conceits, like the *Fire,* or the *Portrait of a Librarian,* which he composed exclusively of books, book marks and a feather duster.

· 16 ·

NICHOLAS HILLIARD
(ca. 1547-1619)

*A Young Man Amidst
Rose-Briars*

Parchment, 5⅜″ x 2¾″
Victoria and Albert
Museum, London

Trained as a goldsmith, Nicholas Hilliard began to specialize in miniature-portraits after 1560. In 1570 he portrayed Queen Elizabeth for the first time and in 1584/7 cut her second large seal. Educated Tudor courtiers cherished miniature portraits, which contrast with the officiality and hieratically removed likenesses of large state portraits. Miniatures were exchanged among the rich because they possessed — according to Hilliard's own treatise on *The Art of Limning* — a "grace in countenance by which the affections appear."

The oval portrait of *A Young Man Amidst Rose-Briars* of the 1580's, exemplifies the intimate character of these exquisite miniatures. The Latin inscription, reading "My praised faith brings my pain," further hints at the sentimental purpose of this likeness.

The young dandy, impeccably dressed, leans pensively against a tree, his slender figure silhouetted against sky and meadow. The delicate filigree of rose branches is played off against the larger shapes of contrasting colors, enmeshing the youthful likeness. Holbeinesque precision has been wedded by Hilliard to an altogether personal delicacy and psychological promptitude. A maximum graphic activity is encapsuled on the surface of a few square inches. Hilliard's pupil Isaac Oliver (died 1617) began to replace the detail of his master with strongly modelled forms, and after his Italian journey of 1596 used colors more in the toned-down manner of oil painting.

ROSSO FIORENTINO
(1495-1540)
and PRIMATICCIO
(1504/5-1570)
Gallery of Francis I
(1534-38)
Chateau of
Fontainebleau

The long gallery of Francis I belongs to the early stages of the architectural transformations at Fontainebleau (1528-32). Since Raphael's *loggia* in the Vatican, long decorated hallways remained a favorite feature of court architecture from Mantua to Versailles.

Unfortunately, nineteenth-century restorers not only raised and replaced the wooden ceiling and the paneling below the decorations, but also repainted Rosso's frescoes and their sculptural frames. A recent cleaning has brought back much of the original work. The subject of these paintings is actually the king himself, whose life is here enlarged upon, and his role identified with examples from antique mythology. Twelve panels fill the spaces between the windows and two more occupy the end wall of the gallery. They are framed with elaborate cornices and sculpture in plaster heightened with gold and inlaid with simulated mosaic.

The overall design of the gallery decorations and the frescoes themselves are largely by Rosso Fiorentino, the stucco sculpture is mainly attributed to Primaticcio who arrived at Fontainebleau in 1532. Many assistants from Italy, France, Germany and the Netherlands figure in the accounts and their contributions may explain the speed with which work progressed. Begun in 1534, it was essentially completed four years later.

A more timid combination of stucco and fresco was also used in Raphael's shop and in Giulio Romano's and Perino del Vaga's work in Mantua and Genoa, but the gallery of Francis I remains distinct and novel in type. Its composite character, ambiguous relationship between fresco, frame, figures of uncertain scale, scroll-work and swags make these decorations prime examples of Mannerist refraction of Renaissance forms.

· 18 ·

NICCOLO
DELL'ABATE
(ca. 1512-1571)
Rape of Persephone
Canvas, 77″ x 85″
Louvre, Paris

Niccolò dell'Abate arrived at Fontainebleau in 1552 as a mature artist, whose training in Modena had left strong traces of Correggio's and Parmigianino's styles. At Fontainebleau he collaborated with his compatriot Primaticcio, and furnished designs for enamel-work, tapestries and festive decorations.

In 1557, payment for four landscape paintings is documented. One of these may very likely be the *Rape of Persephone*. Another picture with *Orpheus and Eurydice* (London) is clearly related in style and format, while the other two pieces seem to be lost. The landscape with the *Rape of Persephone* is built up in layers receding into the distance behind a stagelike foreground silhouetted against the depth. Painted in dashing strokes of cool blue-greens, accentuated by harsh sunlight and muted in the foreground by amber-browns, Niccolò's landscape fuses Italian traditions with impressions of the Antwerp School (Patinier). In the upper right the black horses of Hades' chariot draw Persephone into a gorge to the underworld where she must remain with her husband for four months every year. Her gracefully posed companions on the left recall Emilian painting, while the group of Hades carrying her off seems to anticipate the vigor of Rubens.

· 19 ·

FRANCOIS CLOUET
(died 1572)

Lady at her Toilet

Panel, 36¼″ x 32″
National Gallery of Art,
Washington, D. C.
Samuel H. Kress Collection

François Clouet was made painter and valet of the king's bedchamber after the death of his father Jean in 1541. Probably still a young man then, he later also served Henry II, Francis II and Charles IX. The artist counted many scholars and poets among his friends; Pasquier and the famous leader of the "Pléiade-group," the poet Ronsard, praised him in their writings.

The *Lady at her Toilet* bears the signature FR.IANETII OPVS below the lady's left hand: IANETII refers to his father's name Jean or Janet. This and the portrait of the apothecary *Pierre Quthe* (Louvre), are the only signed works by François. Its impeccable finish, exquisite handling of the different qualities of silk, skin, jewelry and fruit, and its dependence on earlier work by François suggest a date around 1565-70. Many aspects of this work illustrate the composite art of French painters of this period: the half-length figure in the tub is derived from a so-called nude version of the Mona Lisa of which variants by pupils of Leonardo survive, while the contrasting nurse betrays the influence of Netherlandish genre-painting. Finally, the composition as a whole with its curtain setting off the Venus-like nude from a domestic interior, has been derived from Titian's *Venus of Urbino* (Uffizi) of about 1530. But these dependences on Italian prototypes hardly detract from the refined sensuality and peculiarly French tone in elegance and design. The later double portrait of *Gabrielle d'Estrées and her Sister* (Louvre) by an anonymous painter combines the figure of this lady with another one believed to stem from a lost work by François Clouet. Works like the *Lady at her Toilet* ennunciate the more specifically French style of the Second School of Fontainebleau.

· 20 ·

MABUSE (Jan Gossaert)
(ca. 1478-1535)

Venus and Cupid
(1521)

Panel 14″ x 9″
Royal Museums of Fine Arts,
Brussels

Jan Gossaert, called Mabuse, is recorded as a member of the Guild in Antwerp in 1503. The first of the "Romanists" he visited Italy in 1508/9 with his patron Philip of Burgundy and later directed Antwerp painting towards Italianate concepts. After his return from Rome he started to sign his work with a latinized form of his name: Joannes Malbodius. Besides his full-scale mythological paintings, he frequently combined hybrid Late Gothic structures with Italian reminiscences, cast into a strangely lugubrious mood. He also sustained his reputation with portraits and small pieces of religious and secular themes for sophisticated humanists and connoisseurs.

With a playful touch, the uneven group of *Venus and Cupid* (1521) is balanced through an asymmetrical niche repeating the semicircular top of the panel within the frame. Playing off a shape against itself on a different scale is a favorite Mannerist device, e.g. the ambiguity between living bodies and carved statues. Mabuse alludes to this with the shimmering, ivory-like bodies of Venus and Cupid as they break away from the confining niche. An almost ironic note is added with the inscription warning Cupid to spare his mother in order not to perish himself.

46

· 21 ·

PIETER BRUEGEL
(ca. 1525/30-1569)

The Tower of Babel
(1563)

Panel, 45″ x 61″
Kunsthistorisches Museum,
Vienna

The date and place of Bruegel's birth are not known. In 1551 he was accepted as a master in Antwerp, so that a birthdate of ca. 1525/30 may be inferred. In Rome, during his Italian journey he came to know the miniaturist Giulio Clovio — who later also helped El Greco during his stay there — and Clovio's inventory of 1578 mentions a small *Tower of Babel* painted on ivory (now lost); still another small version is now in Rotterdam.

The large version, signed and dated 1563, was painted in the year Bruegel moved to Brussels after his marriage to the daughter of his former Antwerp teacher Coecke van Aelst. In a detached and yet untiringly precise view of the world Bruegel raises the viewer high above the distant horizon, while Nimrod visits the stonecutters in the left foreground. Separated from them by a steep slope, encircled by a contemporary Babel and bordered by the sea, the tower rises from a massive rock in the form of a spiraling ramp towards the clouds, revealing more and more of its vast substructure. The tower has begun to lean towards the left threatening the town, but innumerable small figures are carrying on the toil of building it into the heavens. Late in his life Bruegel was commissioned by the town council of Brussels to record the construction of the canal from Antwerp to Brussels in several pictures, a task for which he seemed ideally prepared had not his death prevented its realization.

· 22 ·

PIETER BRUEGEL
(ca. 1525/30-1569)

The Conversion of Paul
(1567)

Panel, 42½″ x 61½″
Kunsthistorisches Museum,
Vienna

The Conversion of Paul, signed and dated 1567, was copied by Bruegel's sons and other painters. The panel epitomizes Bruegel's late work in its moral view of man's history. Paul's army climbs up through a ravine, encircling and almost hiding the miracle in the middle-ground on the saddle between the two mountain peaks, while rocks and horsemen close the picture from bottom to top at the right. A long, winding movement brings together the distant seascape on the left with the close-up on the right, leading through a world of indifferent vastness.

Related in composition to the *Battle of the Israelites and the Philistines* (Vienna) of some years earlier, Bruegel evolves here a new pictorial concept. Instead of affording a unified and limited view he keeps one's eyes roaming incessantly through the picture. Unable to focus on the miraculous conversion and held at a distance by many figures turning their backs to the beholder, he remains excluded and attracted in a state of bewildered comprehension.

By 1600, both the *Tower of Babel* and the *Conversion of Paul* were in the collection of the emperor Rudolph II in Prague.

47

· 23 ·

LUIS DE MORALES
(ca. 1509-1586)

Holy Family

Panel, 36″ x 26″
The Hispanic Society of
America, New York

Morales died in his home province of Estremadura at the alleged age of 77 in 1586. His work is almost exclusively devotional, centering around the Lord's Passion and the Madonna and Child. Leonardo and his followers in Milan (Luini) and Valencia stand behind the art of Morales, but the Spaniard gave a more mystical character to his panels and also drew from Northern sources. The *Holy Family* in the Hispanic Society is a good example of his Leonardesque endeavor. The *sfumato* and the delicacy of facial features are not entirely matched by the rather hieratic, frontal group reminiscent of earlier icons. In the upper right-hand corner at the side of a burst of heavenly light, Morales has added the horoscope of Christ calculating the birth of the Lord six and a half days before the year one. The horoscope follows Cardano's computation which was published in 1554, but Morales' picture was probably painted in the seventies. Because Morales was painter to the bishop at Badajoz, it seems rather surprising that he dared to add the horoscopes which brought Cardano and other astronomers before the inquisition and eventually into prison.

· 24 ·

EL GRECO
(Domenikos Theotocopoulos)
(1541-1614)

Laocoön

Canvas, 54⅛″ x 67⅞″
National Gallery of Art,
Washington, D. C.
Samuel H. Kress Collection

El Greco's late work is characterized by a visionary fusion of shape and color and a boldness of brush which even surpasses Tintoretto in its feverish intensity. The large size of many of his late works, like the *Resurrection* (Prado) of 1608-10, or the *Clothing of the Martyrs* (according to the Book of Revelation) of 1610-14, and the *Laocoön*, heightens the burning, unearthly quality of his paintings in which bodies in ecstatic gesticulation dissolve their earthbound weight in flaming colors and somber glow clashing with pink and livid hues.

The famous Hellenistic marble group of *Laocoön* which was discovered in Rome in 1506 determined the handling of this theme with almost all painters. El Greco, however, conceived of the tragic group in an altogether original way: set before a storm battered landscape, the writhing bodies of Laocoön and his sons wrestle with the snakes in a deathly struggle watched by a group on the right. The agonized gestures invert the usually heavenbound movements of El Greco's figures as they suffer the revenge of the gods for warning the Trojans of the treacherous wooden horse (seen in the middleground) which the Greeks moved to their city. The landscape of the background recalls El Greco's two *Views of Toledo* (New York and Toledo), but the violent brushwork — in complete accord with the contorted bodies — shapes a vision of terror and tragedy far removed from the ecstatic experiences of El Greco's saints.